Chronicles to Enlightenment

MY PERSONAL JOURNEY TO DIVINE WISDOM

TONI DENT-MCNAIR

NICOLEISH ORIGINALS
PO BOX 4386
FT. MYERS, FL 33918

WWW.TONIDENTMCNAIR.COM

DEDICATION

I dedicate this, my very first book, to the Universe and its Supreme Artistic Creator, God. For, this work is not mine. These words are not my own. Most of this creation was divined by God. My pen was simply the vehicle by which to record His Sacred Truths. These are His words and I honor and appreciate being given the opportunity to impart them to the world.

When I pray, I don't use English words, as most. In fact, rarely do I use words at all. I quietly connect to the harmony of the Universe and tap into the energy that surrounds All. I feel the force. I feel nature. I feel God. Then, I let my heart speak the desires of my soul. The Universe feels and responds in accordance. That is how I may be my most authentic. I just close my eyes and become One with All. And, right now, it is through this silent dedication that I relay my forever gratitude to the Great Spirit.

Having to translate my thoughts into English, obviously for the sake of the reader, my thoughts were this: I thank you for choosing me. I thank you for trusting me. I thank you for empowering me. I thank you. Every word on every page is for You. I love you and thank you for the opportunity to transmit your wisdom to others, as You have so done so to me.

ACKNOWLEDGEMENTS

There are few people in life who bless you and praise you for the uniquely strange yet wonderful person you are. Few people who love and support you beyond all understanding… Few who stretch you and force you to grow beyond your comfort level in order to become a better individual… Few with whom you spiritually develop into One… For the One of whom I speak is my wife, Dr. Joyce Dent-McNair.

I thank my wife for all the mental, physical, emotional, and spiritual support offered to me throughout this process. I also thank her for written contributions as well as the emotional depth entwined into every word she wrote. Dr. Joyce, as she has been affectionately nicknamed, is truly my spiritual Twin. What she thinks, I think. What I am, she is. She is my life and My Love. And, I graciously thank her for all that she is in my life. She is my joy and my inspiration and I thank God for the gift of her. My own growth would surely not have prospered as exponentially as it did had she not been such a colossal presence in my being. I love her more than any words could express. And, I wish her all the health, happiness, and joy any lifetime---every lifetime—can offer.

FORWARD

As we travel along the journey of life, our souls are constantly speaking to us leading us and pointing the way to that beautiful place called home. This type of journey is not for the faint of heart or those who are easily distracted by the negativity, opinions and judgment of those still dwelling in darkness and in unconscious thinking. This is why it is refreshing to meet a soul that is bold enough to go through the process of being broken open in mind, body and soul to the beautiful state of enlightenment. In this book, *Chronicles to Enlightenment* author, Toni Dent-McNair, has laid bare her own path to spiritual enlightenment in a way that invites readers to a safe place of vulnerability and an opportunity to embrace the wondrous journey of self-acceptance, self- love and reminds us that laughter is the key to a merry heart!

My desire for each person reading this amazing written work is to consider the possibilities of a life full of Spiritual wisdom, self-acceptance, joy and a knowing that nothing is happening TO you, but everything is happening FOR you!

I am so glad the Great Spirit led you to this work of art. Get ready to be transformed by the renewing of your mind!

Reya Quarles, M.Ed. Life Teacher,
Co-Author, Educator

TABLE OF CONTENTS

INTRODUCTION

I am love. I have always been love. I shall always be love. We all are and all have been. But, we are born into a world of chaos; one thoroughly contaminated by fear. Fear, in some portions is good and healthy. Some, however, damages the soul. Many do not come back from extreme fear. Others use it as a springboard for finding love and independence. For, this is my story. Experiencing fear made me a warrior. I am strong in my own stance and love beyond human understanding.

I am awakened and alive. Before we awaken, however, we sleep. We do not see ourselves as an astral being, one with the Universe, who now inhabits a body for the purpose of learning and understanding. Through which, we spread and share in God's love and vibrancy. We sleep, living a life in which we perceive ourselves as limited mortal beings who are from earth and placed in dominion over the lands and its "lesser" beings. We believe that which we are taught and settle to accept any position for which we fall within the paradigm.

Funny, I just read a meme on Facebook that said that 90% of humans are sleeping and 5% are awake and desperately trying to wake the 90% up. We won't discuss the other 5%, as they play for the other team…one of negative energy…and I refuse to give any energy towards that in this book. My point is, while I might be a part of the awakened and do ambition to awaken others, the purpose of this book is intended to inspire. By sharing my own personal journey from sleeping to enlightenment, I hope to provide encouragement for others who are perhaps, newly awakened and are walking their own paths. I want to assure them that what they have divined along the way is true and show them what lies beyond their current understanding.

As a child, I used to write divined philosophical sayings. I didn't know they were "divined" so to speak, at the time, but I did know that each was true and that they each instantly emerged in my spirit. That was how I wrote then and how I continue to write today. So, many of my divinings are simply a sentence or two, but are entrenched with extreme depth and meaning. The farther along one gains in the book, the further along one finds in the understanding. You will know where you are in your development based on where your understanding ceases. Once your divine tests are passed and your growth enlightened, then you will understand more in the book.

Shall we begin?

CHAPTER 1

UNAWARENESS

Early Gifts Revealed

As a child of the 70's, I thought I was pretty average. Growing up in a suburban community in Delaware, I had a fairly decent childhood, even though my parents were divorced. Their relationship was amicable, however, if for no other reason than a shared obligation to me. My father was sort of a big deal in our town. He worked as a Director for the State government and reported to the Governor, himself. Having this strong political tie bolstered my family's standing in the community and I, from a young age, knew that I was a member of one of the most prominent African-American families in the State of Delaware, at that time.

Throughout my teenage and young adult years, I struggled to find where I belonged and what my contribution to this world would be. I wrote a lot...mainly philosophical sayings, as I called them back then. I couldn't articulate from where the inspiration came that sparked these sayings but, I knew that they were divined from not my own understanding. However, I received these messages clearly and knew within that what I had written was both true and important. Notebooks holding these early writings have since been lost long ago, however, I do recall one very insightful entry. It read simply, "*Life is too short to die.*" I remember, at twelve, having to explain this passage to those much older than myself. Most translated this to mean the obvious, that life is but a flash and then we, quite literally, die. However, that is not at all what I meant. The word "die" was meant to be figurative. As this passage was divined to me, its meaning was much more dynamic. We are only on this planet for a short while. It is imperative that we make the most of it…that we live to our full potential, as deemed by God…that we rise to every aspect of ourselves in order to fulfill our purpose and the mission given to us by our Creator. I remember feeling so proud of myself when adults asked for my explanation and then so quickly disappointed when they didn't understand it and subsequently dismissed me as some sort of a kook. And soon, the negative responses to my divined knowledge took root in my mind and I began to doubt having this extraordinary gift and settled back into my routine humdrum mundane life.

Bad Girl Revealed

As I aged into adulthood, I gave up on my individuality altogether in exchange for my desire to fit into some subsect of society. I rebelled from the posh life of my adolescence and opted for the life of a Bad Girl. I started drinking…a lot. Peach Cisco was my cheap liquor of choice. Weed and cocaine also became welcome friends. In addition, I also admit that I became much more promiscuous than I ever intended to be. It was never about the sex, though. I, like so many others, was seeking love. I just didn't know at the time that the only source for the magnitude of love for which I sought could only come from inside of me.

Through my 20s-30s, I continued to plummet. I had become lost. My mother died of leukemia when I was 24 and then my grandmother just three years later. Honestly, I think she died of a broken heart due to my mom's passing. Both had meant the world to me since they were the two who mainly raised me. Neither my father, nor any of my half-siblings, offered me the kind of love and support needed by a child who had just lost everything. I felt completely alone. So, in order to assuage the pain of loneliness, I entered into an ill-fated relationship. I moved from sleepy old Delaware to the excitement of New York City to be with my new girlfriend. However, the feeling of unfulfillment followed. There was no love there, just violence and drug abuse. And, as my addiction increased, so did the fighting. I was reaching rock bottom. Inside, I was empty. I hadn't the love from either my family or my girlfriend to validate my worth. And, on the outside, I was bruised and haggard, exhibiting all the traits of someone who was clearly on something and also in an abusive relationship.

Finding Strength

Much like Tina Turner did when she decided to leave Ike after seeing her facial bruises in the mirror; I also had my own revelation that enough was enough. It was as if God, Himself, told me that there was greatness ahead for me if only I had faith enough to trust. That faith grew in me like a cyclone until I clearly saw the new direction of my life. This new inspiration caused me to leave my location, my job, and my ex, in order to recreate a positive life…one focused on healing, positivity, and greatness. So, guided by faith alone, I loaded up my PT Cruiser with only the things that could fit inside and headed as far south as my wheels would take me.

I ended up settling in Naples, Florida. Still driven by faith, I was able to secure a well-paying job within a couple of months. I had no furniture but I had a Bible and an apartment which was more than enough. For, through my Bible readings, I developed a sense of peace that I had never experienced. I knew that I would be alright. I knew that God was with me and that my life was in transition of growing into unknown beauty. At this time, however, I still was unfamiliar with terms like "self-love" or "conscious awareness," but my heart was open and ready to receive. And, oftentimes, that is all that is needed.

Awakening

Inside, I was still in turmoil. For fifteen years, I had endured hell in New York with my ex and had just relocated to a new state. I was alone and desperately yearned for a connection. Emotionally, I was a wreck. I cried a lot. And, I prayed a lot. After one particularly exhausting emotional meltdown, I realized that I could no longer go on like that. I had to pull it together. So, again I prayed to the Universe for help. And, in answering my prayer, the very next day I was divinely called to go to the bookstore to seek guidance. I was lured to the Self Help section and discovered what would be the single most influential book of my life. It was Dr. Wayne Dyer's, *The Sacred Self.* I read it from cover to cover, taking time to practice and absorb all of the lessons for emotional balancing and spiritual growth. From this book, I learned some fundamental truths to self-discovery, including lessons on self-acceptance, ego banishment, the elimination of fear, and silencing the endless chatter within your own head. Of course, it required conscious repetition and positive reinforcement to solidify these foreign concepts into my character. But, as an eager pupil, it seemed to happen very quickly in comparison to the years of misery in which I had been living.

It has been four years since I read that book and I have grown exponentially. Recorded here, in this book, are the lessons I divined on my own path towards personal growth. Each lesson is an individual thought and, these thoughts combined together with the rest have created one authentic body of work. This magnificent work has now become the story of my Journey to Enlightenment.

It is my hope that as you read, that you absorb the full meaning of each passage written. Take in each word until the depth of which correlates within your own soul. Enjoy the ride!

Early Divinings & Humor

1. Love others like you love yourself.

2. There's no way you can be a loving spiritual partner if you don't have the capacity to see into the other person.

3. When you're standing at the mountaintop, you can look down and see what's going on. Those below are the ones who are still struggling. But, from the top, you can see how to help--easily--like breathing. Just reach down and do what you did before.

4. I saw what my mission was today. I'm to help raise up people by getting them to look at themselves, always through love and humor though.

5. I trust you. I trust you with who I am. I trust that you will call me on my bullshit when I'm not being true—or when I'm scared. I trust you.

6. Damn it's cold. Wow! Literally just 2 seconds after I wrote that, there was a whole scene on television about cold fronts. Cool! I love synchronicities.

7. I will be great!

8. I'm not hiding from anyone anymore.

9. My Twin Flame is near and we will lead. I have seen it.

10. I'm watching my cat, Sheldon. I snuck the pen from him that he was playing with, and have started writing. Now, he's watching me write. He knows it's about him. He just touched my hand and laid it on the paper. Yeah, he knows. I love that boy.

11. Pay attention to your advisors. They always have something to say. Mine is furry. Animals can be advisors and protectors, too.

12. I love Family Guy. They say the shit you've always wanted to say.

13. I've noticed that I've been having difficulty jotting down when I'm horny. So what? I've got tingles! I said no more hiding, right? So, I gotta freely reveal everything. And kudos to me for revealing the feeling beyond the feeling.

14. Celebrate who you are. Watch Big Bang Theory. That's who I am…one great big old nerd!

15. Remember when commercials used to make sense? Now, they just say any old stupid shit to get you to buy their products. The sad part is people actually believe this madness.

16. When you see people, you have compassion and then you can help--but only gently…so gently that it's like breathing. You help others by just being yourself.

17. Spiritual Teacher, Gary Zukav, got it right. Read any of his books and you will see.

18. I will dumb down nothing. It is as it is as I understand it.

19. Swearing keeps the muck out. Use it.

20. Raise your awareness. Just do it. You will be great.

21. Why does every movie with an explosion have people just walking away from the fire? If you just went through the trouble to rig some shit to blow up, wouldn't you

wanna watch to make sure that it did that? Just sayin'.

22. Why are people so stupid? They follow along blindly
    while others take the lead. What is it about wanting to be
    a part of the in-crowd that's so appealing? I wanted to,
    too. Can't for the life of me remember why I wanted
    that, though. I flushed through my feelings a long time
    ago. Who even cares what the "why" was for anymore?
    Suffice it to say, the need for acceptance is a mother-
    fucker. People crave it so badly. Instead, be yourself to
    the fullest. Celebrate yourself and others will too. Then,
    you'll be the cool kid!

23. I am proud of me.

24. This is neat how all individual thoughts combining
    together is creating one authentic body of work.

25. Sheldon's not fucking with me anymore. It's like he
    knows I'm doing important work. Whoops, never mind.
    Sheldon! Get down!

26. I've learned the lessons and moved on. It was what it
    was. Everybody's gotta make peace with their shit.

27. I have, as we all have, special gifts. By sharing my gifts, it will allow me to be a leader. I will never again be a follower. Ergo, the only option is to lead.

28. Twin Flames separate to learn and grow, to receive instructions, and to sit with those thoughts only to come back together as a more powerful and a more useful version of ourselves.

29. I want to raise the collective awareness of the entire human race. This is accomplished by creating ripples of illuminated energy. Ripples grow and spread forward into streams of light. If I can spark an infinite number of ripples, this plan just might be doable. It is my mission to try.

30. Be kind. Be loyal. Be noble. Be loving. Be compassionate. Be you.

31. Become love.

32. Why can't lawyers wear jeans and sneakers? That's the guy I want to represent me. It's real. To me, suits and ties are costumes...outfits deemed by corporate America to project confidence and competence. To me, they just say,

"fake."

33. Ritual will not get you closer to spiritual enlightenment.
It's phony. Having rote responses to church passages is
phony. Listless singing of choir songs because the pastor
said it's time for the devotional...it's phony. Saying the
same old prayer before bed is phony. If you're thankful
to God, make sure your praise comes from the heart. Be
authentic with everything.

34. My words are not for those just emerging onto their own
sacred quest of personal awareness. There are many,
including Dr. Dyer, who can help with that. I am here to
tell you what happens next.

35. I am struggling with the last passage because it sounds a
bit arrogant to me. I am committed, however, to share my
wisdom as it was divined to me, devoid of ego. I still feel
completely in-sync though, so I know that it was not a
false statement.

36. I am an admirer of Gary Zukav, who made the following
statement: " It is our duty to grow in order to advance the

human race. That is why we are here. It is our purpose."
Although, not my original words, I agree independently.

37. My equals will know and understand everything I've
written and will meet it with approval knowing everything
I've said to be true.

38. If having a lot of sex is your thing--because you genuinely
like it and not because you're trying to prove
something—cool, have at it. Just be sure to create love in
the midst of all that fucking. It is always about creating
love...authentic love.

39. When you go home (as we are not of this planet) and
look down on all the waves created by your ripples, you
want those waves to be good. You want the effects of
your life to have raised overall consciousness. We are all
here to do our part.

40. Evil is created by muck. When people have so much
muck that all they see is darkness, evil is created. Therein
lies the problem of this planet. There are so many forms
of muck and their manifestations. Hence, there are many
forms of evil. Muck, if left to fester, can eventually lead to
some of the deadliest forms of evil. On the road

downward, we meet self-pity and self-loathing along the way. It is at that point that we must decide to change course or risk the downward decline into the abyss of darkness. It is here where we must intervene and help others to turn back towards the Light. Any longer is too late. Once all you see is darkness, it becomes all you know. The possibility of Light no longer exists without intervening Divine change.

41. Sometimes I want to plug back in to society simply for the entertainment value of it all. People really do some funny shit. There is a warning, though. Only do that once you have grounded yourself and there is no fear of contamination.

42. I can't take it all on a global scale--not the amount of suffering. It hurts too much.

43. Yeah, I will be great. I will be fucking awesome!

44. I keep picking up books from spiritual leaders but they're all like textbooks on how to be happy. It's not authentic. That is why I'm gonna publish this. Nothing has ever been written that's 100% real...every random thought infused with lessons and humor can be truly felt, not just

read. When people feel things, they get it a lot faster.

45. We must show care and compassion for all living things...not just humans--or Americans.

46. Damn, I could go for some Popeye's chicken!

47. I really like me.

48. This has been a really great teaching tool for me. I have learned that I can be intelligent, wise, and funny. I've always known those things but putting stuff on paper adds a whole new perspective.

49. I have lived in and experienced many varied aspects of life. I lived a life of wealth and extravagance but, I have also been broke and hanging out on street corners. I've mingled with some of America's wealthiest socialites but, I've also hung out in some pretty raunchy New York City slums. I've done crazy drugs. I've slept around. But inside, I've always been just me...a genuinely good girl. No one ever saw that, though, so I felt isolated. The point is, I believe I had to have all of those experiences so I could understand the human condition for many of its people. I've lived all this so I may empathize and assist.

50. I have lived my entire life fearlessly. I have done everything up to this point that I have ever wanted to do. Now, I know I can create new goals, mission-based, and I will have an impact. By nature, I have been fearless without even meaning to. So, now I know I can be on purpose.

Chapter 1--Conclusion

As the reader will notice, there were several passages where ego and judgement surfaced. As mentioned, these were some of my earliest writings...those divined closest to the beginning of my journey towards self-discovery. Although the concepts spoken are all truths, as one continues to read they will find the same concepts restated, but in a much deeper and objective way. Keep in mind that the journey lasts a very long time and that deeper levels of understanding are gained along the way. Although I had wisdom at this point, I lacked much understanding. I had not yet grown to a level where I could easily empathize with how others felt nor did I understand why they behaved as they did. I just knew to love everybody.

One will also note that I have included random sub-thoughts amidst my divinations, as well. This document was originally created by writing down all thoughts that were received, in order to appropriately convey its authenticity. It was specifically done solely for that reason...to sincerely capture all thoughts at the time, be they surface or profound.

The final couple of thoughts in this chapter demonstrate growth of awareness by indicating a positive change of purpose and direction.

CHAPTER 2

DISCOVERING I AM

In fleeing from my life of turmoil to my new peaceful world in south Florida, I decided that I wanted to reinvent myself. And, why not? I was in a new state where nobody knew me. I could be who I wanted to be. And, that was to just be myself. But, who was I? What was authentic to my inner core? I had no idea anymore. All I knew was that I had become thoroughly tainted by the years of all the people in my life who constantly yelled my name in anger. From my mother yelling, "TONI!" right before I got my ass whooped to my ex yelling "TONI!" during one of her fits of rage. I loathed that name so much by then that I swore I'd never use that name again. Instead, I chose to start anew by using my middle name, Nicole. I always liked that name better and there was no negative connotation associated with it for me so, Nicole it was. Every person I met, every job application, and even bills and bank records all read Nicole McNair. As I became more comfortable with the name, I started even using variations of it…Nic…Cole…Nicky. Anything was better than Toni. But, who truly was Nicole? Who was Toni? Discovering "the who" inside of "the me" formed my new series of growth spurts.

Divinings Gained Through Self-Discovery

51. When you understand that you just live in this world but aren't of this world, your entire perspective changes.

52. You know you're completely unplugged when you no longer think about how at peace you are. You just are.

53. It's great when you're ok about being different in a sea full of regular. You're not just ok about it but you celebrate it and are grateful for it. It kinda makes you grieve for those who aren't.

53. Whoo, that's one long pubic hair. I gotta cut that.

54. When you get real, you can look at your shit.
    When you look at your shit, you can fix your shit.
    When you fix your shit, you can grow.
    When you grow, you find love.
    And when you love...
    Wow! All things are possible.

55. I can't stand it when my boobs fall outta my bra. I get the right size but I guess they just aren't made with

enough material. I gotta keep stuffing them back in.

56. Oh my God, I just channeled! My right ear started ringing and it was like someone else took over my body. Without thought, I started writing about my own duality. Analyzing it now, I cannot believe how much sense it makes. Thank you, Universe, for helping me to better understand myself.

57. You can stop the suffering when you see it. But, you cannot see it from the level on which it stands. You must rise above to seek its awareness.

58. I am withdrawing into myself. I am tripping about the channeling thing. It was spooky and a bit much. But, I guarantee, 100% authentic. I understood all of my inner psyche at that moment and I still know it. It was different from getting nuggets of wisdom when meditating. My eyes were open. I could talk to the spirit who had entered me. It was loving. It was a soul, but not my own. I don't wanna know right now who it was. I just know it was kind and it was good. That is all I need.

59. You just have to be you at your best.

60. When did Family Feud start asking such ridiculous questions? Seems like they got sillier and more perverted overnight.

61. Sheldon's a genius...not for a cat... but, period.

62. I'm a genius, too. Can't do math for shit but I am, just in other ways.

63. What is this "game" everyone's talking about? Apparently, I have to play some game in order to catch a mate. Isn't that counter-productive?

64. I wonder why slaves followed Harriet Tubman to freedom. She had narcolepsy. I would have thought that would have been too risky. I guess that's what faith is all about.

65. Thank you, Lord, for the gift of humor. Sometimes, it's the best medicine to uplift a People.

66. I wonder why people have issues with folks who post their drama on facebook. It allows the poster to release some muck as well as forces the reader to analyze why they didn't have the balls to do the same.

67. In the beginning, there was God. The Creator. The Ultimate Artist.

68. Oh look! I have a pimple on my butt.

69. People, we need to get our dignity back. Our species is failing rapidly.

70. Can you believe that we, as Blacks, once had to have traveling papers? Think about it. That means that a law was actually made up to say we needed permission from people to walk from one side of town to another. Despicable. We were all born free People. Then the darkness came.

71. It's about being real. But first we've gotta be real with God. Be grateful for All that is first. Then ask him to give you strength to handle the bullshit in your life. However you do it, do it true.

72. Eveline of "The Wiz" is deathly allergic to water. But, she literally sells sweat from a sweatshop. Go figure.

73. I just love nerds, hippies, musicians, and drag queens.

74. Always keep your eye out for inspiration, because it's always there.

75. I am a rebel.

76. Disrefuckinspectable. I shall invent that word.

77. I am strong. I am confident. I am fearless. I am funny. I am creative.

78. People rehash thoughts because they are not living in the present moment and unconsciously begin to "cycle."

79. Damn, I never did cut that long pubic hair.

80. I AM Nicky Mic.

81. Award for best running in a pair of heels goes to Elsa, from *Frozen*.

82. The fakery of it all! Our society is built on it. Stop it, already!

83. Sheldon, are you seriously trying to pop off? You're a cat!

84. There's really a show called, "Amish Mafia"? No indoor plumbing but they've got cocaine and A-Ks. Ok...

85. I need a tissue. My underboob is sweating.

86. I wanna be a drag queen so bad! Those chicks are fierce!

87. Why the hell are gas station bathroom floors always wet? Why can't their clientele ever aim right?

88. I decided to write a letter to my idol, Enlightened Spiritual Teacher, Gary Zukav, to challenge one of his theories. It is as follows:

Hi Gary,

   I've never heard of you prior to last weekend when I saw you on Oprah's "Super Soul Sunday." However, the interview was very interesting to watch because you were saying all the things that I, too, had known to be true. So, it was cool to get that validation. I do have one point of challenge, though. Are you certain that the soul and the ego, or personality as you call it, align? To me, a certain amount of stress develops by constantly checking yourself to make sure you're in alignment. Also, with alignment, theoretically either the soul or the ego can lead, right? Depending on particular stressors or one's state of mind in any given moment. Perhaps enlightenment begins this way, but I believe it should go deeper.

I believe that what eventually happens is absorption, as opposed to alignment. As one goes through the steps in seeking enlightenment, they address every manner of their personality. Once it's all analyzed, we keep the goodness that we know to be true already within ourselves, and get rid of that which is not useful. Although, it is the ego that made us who we are today so we cannot banish it entirely because who we are, in part, rests on that foundation. Instead, the Light of who we are envelops the ego with love. The higher our frequency for love, the brighter the light and the smaller the ego becomes until it dissipates altogether within us. In this theory of absorption, only the soul can ever lead because the ego is no more.

What are your thoughts?

Thank you,
Toni N. McNair

The above was originally written in 2014. It is two years later and I now know that Mr. Zukav and I were saying the same thing.

89. Every negative response is always about the muck that the opposer has within themselves. Always.

90. Recall the moment you initially ingested the muck behind a fear you have. That is the core of the pain. You must dig out the core by releasing the pain. Crying is the way to cleanse muck. Of course, one must be able to identify the fear first. Then, own the resulting opposite positive affect until it becomes naturally one with your psyche.

Chapter 2--Conclusion

In this portion of my walk through Awareness, I discovered the concept of the "I Am." Basically stated, it means that you become whoever you believe that you are. There are no limits to the Great I Am. There are no impossibilities. If I truly believe I am a warrior, my mind, soul, and physical actions work in harmony to perfect who I already know myself to be. It's that simple. So, in my initial discovery of who "I Am," I believed myself to be so funny that I became a stand-up comic. My stage name was Nicky Mic. I was ok, I guess. People laughed. But, after about a year of performing shows, I lost my inspiration. Just as quickly as my intelligence grew and wit came, further growth stunted the things which, formerly, I found to be funny. Previously, my jokes tended toward crass and usually poked fun at random sub-sets of society. As I grew in awareness, however, I gained empathy towards all members of society and judged myself harshly for even thinking such unloving thoughts toward others. This internal criticism created resistance in my body and I became blocked. It took me almost two years to accept that due to loving growth and understanding, I would no longer be a stand-up. Instead, I would use my humor, along with my many other talents, as a part of a larger mission...one that would heal and not destroy. I believe this is that work.

I chose to end this chapter when I did because the block I experienced could be seen in my writing at the time. Many of the statements were more forced comedic bits, fueled by ego, with no spiritual value, than they were authentic divinings from the Universe. So, it was apropos to conclude there.

CHAPTER 3

TWIN FLAMES

As I continued to spiritually grow, I deepened the love I had for myself, for others, and for the world. I developed such a vibrancy that I began to notice that I seemed to be positively affecting others around me. People who once had hatred in their hearts now exhibited inner lights of their own. I was happy. Indeed, I was joyous.

There is a theory that proposes that when a spirit is ready, its Twin Flame will appear. Twin Flames or Twin Souls represent a dynamically spiritual union between temporarily separated souls who join together on Earth for an elevated divine purpose. To be "ready" to receive one's Twin, one must live mostly through the Self and have taken conscious steps toward ego elimination. One must also be mentally prepared to accept the challenges that such an intense relationship presents. While there will be intense physical and mental emotion, there will also be some intense battles. These battles, however, are merely spiritual tests designed to decrease the ego and grow one's capacity to love. If successful, a growth spurt occurs and further awareness is gained.

I guess I was ready because, during this time, I met the love of my life...my Twin Flame. Many of the divinings received during this period pertain to her and this intensely beautiful love that we share. Her name is Joyce (JD) and I met her online. That is all I will say on that. Rather, I prefer that our love be experienced through the divinations.

Through my journals, I have written about my whole spiritual process. This chapter is dedicated specifically to the experience and learnings and truths of the inner knowledge of being a part of a Twin Flame Experience. Everyone wants it but not everyone has learned the power needed to manifest one. It's a gift that God gives once we are on the road to completing our inner work. Do the work needed. Be as Christ-like as you can. Your Twin will come.

The divinations within this chapter were received from when we first corresponded online through our first two years together.

Divinings Gained Through Twin Love

91. I don't know you, but I love you.

92. I am in love with a woman I've never met. We've only chatted online. How did this happen? I know...and I thank you, Lord.

93. We raise each other up and love each other in the exact way we each need to be loved.

94. You were just telling me about how it was when they integrated New Orleans. Literally five minutes later, "Ruby Bridges," the story of an African-American girl who integrated a New Orleans school came on television. Synchronicities are awesome!

95. I believe we are two parts of the same whole, but not a straight half and half. Parts are more jagged. But, when we reunited, we perfectly fit together.

96. We so complement each other equally. Where she is more dominant, I am less. Where I am more, she is less. It is instinctual. It is our cosmic make-up.

97. Life is amazing and God is awesome!

98. Human love makes your heart beat fast and out of balance. Cosmic love makes your heart still, calm, peaceful.

99. I'm in love. Simply. Purely. Honestly. Wholistically— Love.

100. Human love falls in love with the fake. Once the façade is gone and the real is exposed, people can't handle it anymore because, in actuality, it was never the "real" that they wanted in the first place. They are fake so they get fake in return. Like attracts like—The basic Law of Attraction. That is why the divorce/break-up rate is so high. It only works if couples grow at the same time, together…learning. They continue to stay at the same level together.

101. Twins come to each other already prepared for the real. It's instinctual. No games. No masks. Just total trust and total vulnerability. It just is.

102. People meet soulmates all the time. They are the ones who teach the life lessons to each other and work

together to grow. Twins have already learned God's Laws of Love and are whole unto themselves...for the most part, no longer fractured within their selves. They are each a complete ONE. But, we come here as TWO—two complete souls conjoined as one love, one whole. We separate to each increase the flow of energy and light and when our lights are brilliant, we come back together to create one ultra-brilliant glowing ray of light. Only together can they grow continuously, each quietly lovingly helping the other to be their best and brightest selves.

103. Animals are better than humans in that they already know this stuff. I've never seen a white cat not accept a black one. Their love is based on good or bad feelings about another.

104. You know when things are authentic because your heart is still...calm...peaceful...because the knowledge came by God, Himself.

105. God is Great!

106. "I am appreciative of every atom of your being." –JD

107. "If Jesus is my joy, you are my happiness." –JD

108. Let's talk about cursing. They are human English words. God cares not—only about the intention. If you swear without malice and it is the embodiment of who you have become on Earth, then it's cool. It's who you are. But, if there is anger in your words—any of them, including swear words, then it's bad and you infect your heart.

109. My beloved has a chronic sleep disorder, but she sleeps when she is with me. She is at peace.

110. I believe that I have perfectly incorporated all of who I am with who I AM. Anything that doesn't fit, Joyce will point out for me. That is what spiritual partners do. And, I am grateful for everything she points out, no matter how uncomfortable it is.

111. What if you were Adam and I was Eve and, as my sworn mission to God to correct my original mistake, I chose to come back during each major generation to undo fear and sow love. Because Adam loved me so much and also yearned to sow love, you joined me in this mission. And, in each generation, we find each

other. That is why we fell in love so quickly…because, in actuality, it wasn't quick at all.

112. The more fractured one is, the more one is out of alignment. And, conversely, the more balanced one is, the more aligned. The higher the level of balance, the more enlightened. This explains everything from finding wholeness to the multi-disorders of the highly damaged.

113. You are the rhythm of my heartbeat, my shelter in the midst of my storm, my raft in my stormy seas, my ray of light in my darkest journey. You were created by God for me only. Never have I been moved by such a love or a presence as this love. The word, "love" even seems to be too small to describe what I am feeling. It will take all of Heaven and Earth to contain this love portion held for you. But, for your smile to grace upon me I, myself, will move all of Heaven and all of Earth. For, that smile has caused me to stand still and absorb what real love is meant to be. I love you. If I had one wish, I could wish for nothing more than to rise each morning with you in my arms. –JD

114. I miss you. I miss everything about you. I swear, I

could get lost in the nape of your neck forever, just
bathing in your scent.

115. "The thought of kissing feverishly your lips
       has dominated my thoughts." –JD

116. During an evening of texting between us:

Me: I am listening to Kem's, "It's You." and I am
            smiling because…it IS you.

JD: My heart just melted a li'l…damn, you can
            make me smile.

Me: Don't let it melt too much. I want the whole
            thing. I love that I can make you smile. I
            love you, Joyce.

JD: My heart has been yours since we first spoke.
            I am aching to hold you right now.

Me: Me too, Baby. Me too. Goodnight, My Love.

JD: I am at peace with you in my life. Goodnight,
            My Angel.

117. She is here with me now and it feels like home. I love
     her so much and I am so grateful. Thank you, God,
     for saving me. I never could have thought that
     reciprocal love was so dynamic—so magnificent. I've
     never experienced anything like this—anything close

to this. There is nothing wrong…like, nothing…
nothing that works my nerves and nothing
that's out of place. Who she is perfectly fits with who I
am. We are the same—Twins.

118. You let the people in that you care about. But, in
doing so, you can also allow the things that these
people say affect you adversely. In doing so, you can
become infected and, consequentially, lash out and
become venomous towards others. I choose not to
become infected ever again.

119. We are all Divine loving energy at our core. That is all.
Anything else is ego.

120. My favorite Teachers are Rumi, Buddha, Tesla, Thich
Nhat Hanh, Dr. Wayne Dyer, Lao Tzu, the Dali
Lahma, and Gary Zukav.

121. I can totally be myself with her. It's nice.

122. Basic rule… I won't be unkind to you and you won't be
unkind to me. Sure, we'll have slip ups but, if we always
remember that we love each other then, we won't take
anything personally. Our love for each other will

always prevail.

123. Aw, she thinks I don't like the person that she is. I've
      gotta do a better job showing her that I don't just like
      her but, I love her. Yes, Baby, I do like you…very
      much. You're fun. You're funny. You have such a
      giving heart. You're a smart-ass. You're pleasant and
      have a welcoming smile. You're polite. You're
      country fun. And, you have this innocence about you.
      You are fabulous! A perfect fit. Yes, Baby, I like you.

124. To know someone is to "see" someone. To see them
      is to understand them. To understand them is to love
      them.

125. We are about 5 ½ months in now and it's lovely. We
      are perfect in that that which we are not perfect about,
      we correct it—for the other as well as for ourselves so
      that we may be perfect. I love this woman so
      much…so much that the room gets lighter and I just
      burst with energy for her. I thank the Lord for this
      reuniting.

126. I love you like I love myself.

127. Our joint mission is to spread love across the masses. She is great in that she can spread her love across those who are most wounded. I don't have that gift. I have tried but the pull into darkness proved too strong for me. So, I seek to help those who are ready for growth and change. I commend her. She truly is talented at her craft.

128. She suits me.
    I wear her smile as an adornment of favor.
    My love is for her only.
    She suits me. Her eyes illuminate my way as I find my search for her and her alone.
    She suits me. Though I am of flesh and bones, it is her lobe that I wear as I may attest.
    She suits me. –JD

129. I keep replaying making love to you and how you just take my breath away. I love you. –JD

130. You are my life, Joyce. The reason I had to endure all the bullshit from my youth. They were all lessons I had to endure…all my preparation for you. I came to you as polished as I could. I will ask you to continue the work of helping me to shine as vibrantly as possible. I

smile as I continue this journey with you. You are my life.

131. Mi Bella, I live in adoration of your beauty. I am renewed each day by the warmth of your love. My day begins and ends on the joy of your smile. I adore you. –JD

132. Your love is the treasure that many spend a lifetime or more in search of. Yet, I have found you for many lifetimes to come. I love you. –JD

133. I honor you. Honor me. Let your ego go, Babe. It's ok. I love you. Be who you truly are…your soul. Align, Baby, align to your highest Self. I love you. It's ok.

134. We are beginning to communicate telepathically which, is a hallmark of Twins. No sooner than I wrote the preceding thought, I saw her alignment begin. I thank you, Lord.

135. We have a physical, emotional, mental, intellectual, and spiritual attraction.

136. She is my King and I am hers. She is my Queen and I am hers.

137. Cleaning off muck gives one clarity. The more you clean, the better you "see."

138. Nothing external will ever get rid of the muck. There is only one way...you have to climb out of it from the inside.

139. I see collective suffering and it's disturbing. I feel it in my chest. My heart starts beating profoundly. This is why I cannot watch some television shows. I see it not as an individual walk but as a collective mass of damaged people and it is painful to see. I feel it physically in my body. I feel empathy.
The way this manifests in human life is that I can see if someone is a good person or not. All of us have bits of muck on us. Some of us may be waist deep. Some may be up to their chins. As long as there are parts that can still see the light shining above the muck, then there is still hope that they can climb out. All it requires is a margin of strength, hope, and faithfulness. Unfortunately, those who are totally submerged have

surrendered the light and given in to the darkness. That is, until something cracks them open and allows the Light to shine in.

140. When you are quiet, you can feel the vibrational direction of your heartbeat. Is it calm or beating vigorously? If it's beating hard, you are outside of your vibrational path. That means it's time to re-group and re-center.

141. Human society has been made up by ego-driven damaged people who, in order to feed their egos, manipulate the energy to swing to their direction. This manifests by making others feel inferior in order to be led by those who believe themselves to be more powerful. It is all a façade. Take your own power back. Be who God intended you to be.

142. I awoke looking for my love to enter my door…
With her eyes full of joy to be reunited and her smile all ablaze just for me.
I shall rest here until she returns…
I awoke looking for my love to enter my door ---JD

143. Forever I could kiss you.

Forever I could hold you.

Forever I could lie with you.

Forever I could make love to you.

Forever I could stare into your eyes.

Forever I could admire your smile.

Forever could I stay in your embrace.

Forever could I laugh with you...talk with you...be with you...admire you...honor you.

Forever I will love you. Forever...

144. April 17, 2015, I married my best friend and her name is Joyce.

Chapter 3—Conclusion

The main function of Twin Flame love is to increase self-awareness and promote soul growth, thereby, removing the barriers which are blocking the deeper love we have within. It was important to share the letters written between my beloved and me because the depth of love can be so immensely felt. And, there is no true way to thoroughly describe love, especially one so intense. It must be personally felt in order to be understood. That is why writers write...to attempt to vividly describe emotion to those who may not have experienced it. The difference here is that these are not just writings but original letters professing a purely strong and unrestricted love for the other. The most radical and expedient growth can be obtained through one's participation in a Twin Flame relationship. By nature, these relationships force us—through love—to become more patient, understanding, and kind. Our souls grow through self-examination. It is my honest wish that those whose spirit is strong and pure enough to receive it are offered the opportunity to reunite with their Twin. Though not without its heartache, as soul growth often is, it is the most magical and lovingly intense experience one could ever endure.

CHAPTER 4

ALIGNMENT & BALANCE

Alignment occurs when the ego vanishes and the most genuine aspects of yourself join in syncopation with your Godly spirit. The Duality of the Selves dissipates and we become One with the Universe. When we are aligned, peace reigns from within and our true Self becomes dominant. Once we align within ourselves, we become balanced with all that is. Our inner peace radiates outward and love and joy remain constant interior sensations, despite any outside negative influences. We feel God's presence at all times and stay in a total state of gratefulness for All that is. Even at this moment, I want to stop and thank God for this wonderful gift of Life and for being chosen as a conduit for conveying His Universal Truths.

Through balance, Focus enhances. There is no more consciously planning to be consciously aware. One just is, at all times. We become unconsciously conscious. And, it is through this state that the remainder of this book is written. There will be no more random sub-thoughts sprinkled through the divined teachings but simply the teachings themselves. Focus allows us to stay on task and absorbed into every moment. For, as I became more perfectly balanced, so did my Focus. And with deepened Focus, we can hear the Universe speak so profoundly…and so truthfully…and so mightily Holy.

When Balanced, the Universe speaks to all of us. We must only quiet ourselves enough to listen. The following divinings are Universal gifts of truth and wisdom from God. Still your minds, focus on the words, and absorb their meanings in your heart. And you, too, will feel God's truths for yourselves.

Divinings Gained Through Balance & Focus

145. Body is an inanimate object that we, as the life force, animates. The life force moves throughout the body causing all to be alive. When the life force leaves, the body disanimates.

146. The opposite of the emotion of love is fear. But, the opposite of the feeling of love is pain. And, all four can change people.

147. I believe that you can create through either complete devotion to Self or complete devotion to personality. We choose whether we want a life of Light or of dark. When we align, we take our best aspects of our personality and intertwine it with our Higher Self.

148. When you merge into alignment, your ego teaches your Self how to protect itself.

149. One can have a flair for the darker aspects of life without bringing in the darkness.

150. There are varying depths of Love. And, this is the deepest that I have experienced, thus far.

151. The right-brain houses our Self and our Divine Universal Knowledge. The left-brain houses our ego and our Earthly concepts. Merge the two and there we find balance. Balance is the key to unlocking our Divine Power.

152. Good looks and great sex is not a reason to get married. Marriage without a soul connection makes divorce inevitable.

153. We all have the power to affect. Why not affect with joy and happiness as opposed to infecting with hate and negativity? Let's make the world better.

154. Only the things that we give power will have power.

155. People are going to judge you. The key to happiness is to genuinely not care that they do. Be You. Always.

156. Live in the space between the thoughts.

157. My deepest desire in this life is to be appreciated for my beauty…inner, never outer. I want to affect massive positive change just by being myself.

158. Love equals attention. The more focused attention given towards something, the more genuine the experience.

159. Always meet aggression with love to create a positive change. Aggression will only create more aggression.

160. When faced with a challenge, choose the course that makes your heart still—calm. Your body will always tell you the right course of action.

161. There's not just one way to do anything. If you do something while in your perfectly balanced state, you will master it perfectly in your particular way, which is magnificent. Do not judge yourself about what you think should be. Whatever you are, is.

162. One must be genuinely inspired in order to achieve aspirations.

163. Seek clarity.

164. We should have three passions which become our life's work:

The first should be something that fuels your
own soul.
The second should be something that fuels
the souls of others.
The third should be something to fuel the
soul of the world.

It's up to you to discover what they are. Don't look too
hard. They are the things that you already naturally do.

165.   You ever just watch the birds fly in formation? It's
very beautifully choreographic and symmetrical.

166.   There are three internal steps to solidify growth:
First, the soul receives the message from the Universe
and processes and internalizes it. Secondly, the left-
brain (ego/personality) accepts and internalizes the
same message, as it relates to earthly life. Then, lastly,
both sides merge and accept and solidify the lesson
together. That is wholeness.
This process is usually preceded by a period of internal
struggle or pain, the length of which is directly related
to one's current level of awareness.

167.   We always get signs. We just have to pay attention to
see. Life is filled with them. Synchronicities are signs

that we are on the right path.

168. I am grateful. This has been a phenomenal year, Lord. I thank you and I love you.

169. Always say what you mean. Instead of "Namaste," I shall say, 'I honor you." Namaste has become another colloquial word used simply because others use it so carefreely. Be original 100%.

170. What if the smallest size of us is the life spark itself? If so, through challenges, we must continually and consciously grow that spark into a full and magnificent beam of radiant light. The darkness asks us to diminish that spark until it is no more. Through luminosity, as one spark shines brighter, its radiance affects others and creates an even brighterness within them as well. The lighter our own spark, the bigger its glow, and the more radiance we emit into the world. Light up the dark!

171. I am free. I live in no one's bowl.

172. We each will when we will, but we will.

173. Words can be used for judgement or for truthful speak. If your heart is truly and fully one of love then, words mean nothing. Even the foulest of words are meaningless if the heart is pure. The meaning is in the intention, not the translation. The words themselves are simply a human construct.

174. The world needs awkward. Be you always.

175. Even the smallest ant deserves life. Kill nothing.

176. When we are off-balance, we are unwhole. Our personalities separate. Depending on how off-balance we are determines how far we separate. For me, my most immature personality appears.

177. Strength comes from peace, not war. Earthly power comes from war, and the two are nowhere the same.

CHAPTER 5

REACHING ENLIGHTENMENT

How do I know I have attained a certain amount of
enlightenment? I've asked myself this question several times.
I never want to appear boastful or entitled or incorrect in my
speech…but then, I focus my thoughts on God. My heart is
still and my mind quiets. As my eyes tear with love, my soul
feels at peace and I know that God has answered my
question. I am grateful to know that He is pleased with my
development, thus far. I still have much to learn and far to
grow but I know that I am on the right path. Most of my
muck stains have washed away and I feel the brightness of
Light within me shining through at all times. I am love…and
I feel it every moment of every day.

Through enlightenment, we can see the world from
the highest human level. We see life and the human
condition clearly for what it is…both the good and the
bad…and understand why it is so. Through understanding,
we can make changes for the betterment. This has always
been a major fallacy of the world. Laws affecting others have
simply been made, based off human opinion, without any
effort given to understanding the full plight of those to whom
the laws have affected. Understanding, however, is a key trait
of the enlightened. We can see others because our hearts are

opened to do so. It is here, in this state, where we can positively affect the most change on humanity. Enlightenment is a gift from God and, by combining this gift with our own inherent humanly gifts collectively, we can uplift a People and save a world.

For now, I shall end the commentary and just write. The divinations and teachings are abundant and the actual focus of this manual. Though, this is my story, the words on the pages belong to God. This was always the intent ...to pass along God's Universal Truths. For, this is and always was His book. I am simply the conduit. So, with peace, love, and honor, I shall remove myself and let the Universe speak directly to you.

Divinings Gained Through Enlightenment

178. Do everything through truth, love, and humor.

179. Strength, fueled by Light wins. The more Light, the more strong of Spirit.

180. My relationship with All is a direct effect of my relationship with God.

181. What was, what now is, acceptance of what now is, complacency, evolution and the unveiling of false truths, revolution, and peace. This is the cycle of life. Currently, we are entering the Revolution phase.

182. Levels of Consciousness equal Focus Levels. The lower the focus level, the more separated the personality and therefore, unfocussed on the present which causes loss of the spirit. Total focus is the art of being unconsciously conscious 100% of the time.

183. People tend to speak from two places, their head and their heart. If we listen closely, we can hear them speak from both. Our goal, rather, should be that both

become the same.

184. I don't understand embarrassment or offense. Both are interpretive responses. When one speaks loving truth, the intent is to cause neither.

185. We have to understand the darkness in order to gain empathy. And, in order to understand it, we have to experience it. That is the order of things. It is a part of the system needed to grow and gain balance. Equally, we must deepen our cultivation of love, as well. As our love strengthens, we can affect those suffering in the darkness through our experiences by bringing Light.

186. Truth in ourselves brings authenticity.
      Authenticity brings love.
      Love brings spirituality.
      Spirituality brings peace.
      Peace brings balance.
      Balance brings Light.
      And Light heals the world.

187. Only the weak need to look strong. The strong have no need to advertise it.

188. As you grow more, you know more.

189. These things I know—

    1. The Creator is Most Holy.

    2. The Universe superbly loves and supports us.

    3. True and Unhindered Love is the most powerful force in existence.

    4. We are here to spread Light.

190. Always be authentic with God. Do not beg but be calm with your prayers. Speak from the smallest and innermost part of your heart. There is from where you are sincerest in your Truth.

191. Be so filled with Light that you can balance yourself midway between Light and dark, Heaven and Earth.

192. When perfectly whole, you will feel like air. No resistance from anywhere. You will feel love and peace with All.

193. You can tell how much darkness is in a person by the amount of eye contact diverted. Direct eye contact equals focus. They are focused on you and, therefore, listening and spiritually connecting with you. In that

moment, they are giving and receiving love. And, Love is Light. When eye contact is diverted, they are not focused on Truth and therefore, not in connection with you or the Spirit. Since focus equals love, in this instant, there can be no pure love. And, where love lacks, fear thrives. Fear initiates darkness.

194. Accept what is. Have confidence in knowing that what is will continue until corrected. Then, expect it each time the same occurs. Once you can expect something to occur, you can plan your response in advance. You've already accepted it so you have peace in it. So, your response will be peaceful.

195. There is something deeper than love. Understanding. However, it's cyclical. Through understanding, we gain deeper measures of love.

196. Balance leads to focus. Focus leads to love. Love leads to understanding.

197. When one is fully balanced, one is fully in faith with God…always grateful and always loving. That is what God wants. When we are fully absorbed with the Holy Universe, we are also in balance with all that is All.

That is when our Light shines the brightest. The more vastly and vibrantly we shine, the more we affect Love towards others.

198. Accept where you are and then improve.

199. Fear is an overwhelming infection spread from spirit to spirit through every interaction. If it is not recognized when it enters our bodies, it will cause a stain on our souls. So many ingest and keep so much fear inside that their spirits are completely tarnished and begin to wither away. That is why it is so important to learn the tools of self-love in order to cleanse ourselves of this fear. The clearer our spirits, the more Light we allow in which, in turn, clears more tarnish...and so on. Through Light, we not only heal ourselves but, as it gains vibrancy within us, heals others as well.

200. There are three kinds of people: those with no emotions, those with fluctuating emotions, and those with complete balance of all. Strive for the last. For, that is where the power lies. Magic is found in the state of complete balance.

201. The greatest atrocity in the history of the world is how evil has taken root and infected the planet. Its manifestation has resulted in a divisive strategy to instill fear in all lifeforms in order to secure domination for a select group of its followers. Thankfully, God's People are now awakened.

202. Let us not forget the lessons from the past but, take forward our newly learned knowledge so not as to repeat the past. The time is now to change our destiny.

203. Love is pure.

Love is kind.

Love is patient.

Love is true.

Love is innocent.

Love is Beauty.

Love is Understanding.

Love is Air.

Love is Breath.

Love is Hope.

Love is Holy.

Love is Nature.

Love is Life.

Love is All.

204. Balance is perfection. It is the key for conquering the darkness. For, the level below balance is duality. Our Light side and our dark side…our loving side and our fearful side…both contain ego. When we rise to the level of balance, however, we rise above our egos and hence, above the darkness. Without dark, there can only be Light. Defeat the darkness. Choose Light.

205. During each subsequent lifetime, we must clear the karma from the preceding life. That is how we grow through generations. What your greatest fears were before, sometimes even stemming from death, will resurface during the next lifetime asking us to see and acknowledge the lesson so we may make different choices in subsequent lives.

206. I am not what I am on the outside. I am who I am in me. It is important to know the difference.

207. Sometimes it is helpful to remember that people are doing the best that they can and that we're all growing to be better, if even incrementally.

208. Becoming angry is a choice. Like all negative behavior, it is learned and not inherent. Thus, it can be eliminated.

209. Anything not of God is fake. Fight the fake.

210. Darkness is created by those who don't know love. But, once you know love, you'll love Love.

211. Why has man determined that some rocks are less valuable than others? God did not say to value the diamond over the ruby or the ruby over the pebble in the forest. Just because man does not see the beauty of each individual of nature does not mean it is not so. Even the grain of sand has beauty and value.

212. In all things, always choose the most loving response.

213. When it's pure and true, it's significant.

214. We must have hardship in order to crack. We must have cracks in order to break. And, we must break in order to find our strength to survive.

215. Like the moon, enlighten what is dark…both in

yourself and in others.

216. The world needs real. It's screaming for it...crying for it...dying for it.

217. It is one thing to clean the windows and quite another to shine the glass. Plan to sparkle!

218. Eliminate fear and find confidence. Confidence equals magic.

219. Recognize spiritual solutions to solve human problems.

220. Walk with certainty...not oblivion...but certainty.

221. Send every entity Light. Do not condemn. Do not hate. Seek to understand the evil in the world and then consciously and genuinely send the darkness love.

222. Be brave. Take chances. The only one stopping your advancement is you.

223. Breaking is never to our detriment. Rather, it is the process which encourages soul growth.

224. As our fear wanes, our power grows.

225. Balance + Focus = Positive Manifestation.
Ego + Focus = Negative Manifestation.
The power is in the Focus. The result comes from the intent.

226. Let the peace from God shine from above through you to the Earth below and then radiate far and wide. This is the real Holy Cross.

227. Living in the present allows Balance. Balance allows Focus. Focus allows manifestation. Keep your Focus good and good things will manifest.

228. The size of your ego often equates to the amount of muck contained inside.

229. When we grow, we move closer into alignment. With closer alignment comes a closer love for oneself and others. Therefore, feelings of anger and negativity dissipate sooner.

230. It's about Life. We must save Life. And, in order to save Life, we must increase our collective awareness and grow. When we grow, we expand our Light to illuminate others…and when they grow, they shine their lights…and when those grow…and so on.
That is how we save the planet. We must save the soul of the Earth because she is dying. And, just like we receive healing energy from our friends and loved ones when we are sick…think about how much is needed to save our Mother. The good news is that we have God on our side.

CHAPTER 6

ENLIGHTENMENT MANIFESTED

Stand Up!

If there is a cause in your heart to stand up for—a cause that you know in your core is for right—then now is the time to act. If it is a justice needed or a help provided that has not yet already been established, then create it. Be your own individual force for change. Your unique contributions are needed.

Freedom Fighters

Freedom Fighters are everywhere and I love it! They are fighting for all facets of life against evil. Some fight against politics. Some fight against enslavement. Some fight for equality. Some fight for the Earth. Some fight for Humanity. And, some fight for all of Life in general. We are a Team fighting in unison for Right. And, I love to see it All.

My Mission

Through God's infinite Light and Wisdom, I will work to raise the collective consciousness of all humanity.

Your Soul Purpose

Through balance, love, truth, and understanding, work to positively contribute to humanity using your own unique gifts. This is not only desired but it is required. The world needs every one of you. Life, itself, needs you. Do not squander the talents that you have been given. They were given to you for your Soul Purpose. There is no better and no greater expression of gratitude to God than to use that which you have been given to uplift the People and to manifest Universal holiness here on Earth. Your time is now.

Eliminate Use of the Phrase, "I Can't"

The term, "I can't..." is limiting and false. We can change anything about ourselves that we desire. We must first clearly decide what it is we want and then meditate/pray/download the new programming from the Universe. This will allow our subconscious mind to receive knowledge and recognize signs pointing to what it is we want. Eliminate the "can'ts" from your vernacular and then everything can become possible. We just have to decide what it is we want. This theory is not unlike Neo in *The Matrix* when he wanted to learn judo. He desired the knowledge, requested the program, practiced, and became a master. Trust that the Universe can do this for you, too, if you so desire. A positive attitude and the knowledge of what "I can" can do, allows the Universe to grant you anything.

Do No Harm

My religion is simple. God has one binding law that covers all—Do No Harm. That is my guiding doctrine. Harming anything of Life damages the natural intent of God as well as the being itself. Harming pollutes because it does not allow for complete Freedom of the Soul to develop as intended. So, let the rock be. Do not pick the flower. Do not encage the lion. And, do not enslave the man.

Patience

Sometimes, you just have to let time do as time does. It changes your situation. The interesting part is finding out if it is for the better or not. The more noble your cause for change, however, the more of a chance it'll be.

Praying

When you pray, be authentic with your prayers. Talk to God like you would your best friend. Forget the memorized canned prayers that society has taught you to say. Speak to the Universe from your heart. Be 100% authentic 100% of the time. Be honest, do you even know what 'hallowed be thy name" means? And, even if you do, do you naturally even talk like that? If the answer is no, then how could it possibly be real?

Emotions

Emotions are a choice. Reprogram yourselves to drop all emotions except for Love. For, the longer the emotion held, the more off-balance we are. Continuing to replay a thought-driving emotion means we are cycling and, therefore, stagnating in our growth. Conversely, when a thought emerges at the same time the emotion does and then it instantly dissipates, we find balance.

Changing the Channel

When we are practiced in complete Focus, we can easily change our energetic frequency to, instead, divert attention to that which we desire. Our minds no longer distract so negative or disturbing thoughts become obsolete…as does pain and sleepless nights.

Harmony

There is a natural harmony and flow of Life and we are to be One with it. Never push or force things. That energy is speedier than what is in balance with nature. Rather, harmonize with it. Feel its peace…its resonance.

Chapter 7

THE TWELVE LAWS OF KARMA DEFINED

The Great Law

Ancient Asian teachings define karma as the spiritual manifestation of cause and effect. It is the spirit in which one thinks, speaks, or behaves that is returned to the doer. Should one speak love then love is spoken of them. And conversely, should one's motivation be of hate then hatefulness is returned upon them. For what is given must be received. This theory is known as The Great Law or, as it is more widely known, as the Law of Cause and Effect. It is real. And, it is Universal. Be good and receive good. Show deceit and deceitfulness will be shown unto you.

The Law of Creation

We are One with the Universe as an active energetic member seamlessly intertwined with all of Life itself. We are no more nor less important than any other member of God's creative force. Because of this union, we are able to transmit our thoughts into the wind and allow them to be carried and responded to by Creation. Thus, through co-Universal creation, we manifest active thought into reality. That on which we supremely focus becomes created so it remains important to only think good and loving thoughts in order to produce good and loving things.

The Law of Humility

We must let go of that which we wish would be and accept that which is. Once we accept what is, we vanquish a part of our ego and growth occurs. Acceptance is devoid of judgment and thereby allows love and patience to flow from within.

The Law of Growth

It is imperative that we, as sentient beings, expand in betterment of who we are. Our Self is the only thing over which we have power. And, through power we can make changes. But first, we must be able to see who we are before we decide that a change must be made. This comes through self-awareness. Once we can closely examine ourselves, we can find our flaws and fix them. We can become better. For, it is not others who need changing…it is us. And, when we become better, we perceive others as better too.

The Law of Responsibility

We are all a product of our choices therefore; we must be liable for the choices we make. Blame does not exist as it is perception-based only. Our perception of what is real is subjective. So, it must be us to whom we hold accountable for the decisions we make, both good and bad. And, through acknowledgement of both, we grow.

The Law of Connection

All occurrences combine to form outcomes. Each seemingly small thing joins with other seemingly small things all in pursuit of larger advancements. Nothing is random. Every piece and part of Life is connected. No deed is greater or lesser than any other. For, all is necessary to create the greater masterpiece of our lives.

The Law of Focus

It is imperative that we, as individuals, learn the skill of Focus. Through Focus, manifestation occurs. However, one must be balanced to achieve Focus. Without balance, our personalities are split. Thus, so is our vision and focus. We become scattered and, therefore, cannot steady ourselves enough to seek clarity of vision. It is also impossible to focus on more than one thought at a time. When we are balanced, however, we quiet our minds to naturally focus on each present moment. If we stay focused on Love, Love will reign in our lives.

The Law of Giving & Hospitality

Many say that they care about others but it is in the action that proves a person's character. All spiritual doctrines cite the importance of caring for our fellow lifeforms and it is in the heart of each lifeform to inspire good in others. This Law should not be entered into out of obligation but rather due to our natural desire to care for another's well-being. For giving, itself, is a gift. Give to others unsparingly. There is great joy and peace in doing so.

The Law of Now

Neither the past nor the future can affect us if we don't let it. For, each moment is a gift to be enjoyed. Plus, Balance, Focus, and Manifestation can only be achieved when one is totally immersed in the Present. Thoughts of regret or worry are products of past or future concerns, neither of which are conducive to growth and, both representative of fear, at its root. And, where there is fear, love cannot flourish. For, neither can occupy the same space. Love is the product of Now.

The Law of Change

We cannot change what we do not see and we cannot see what we choose not to accept. Therefore, acceptance is key. Similar to The Law of Growth, we must accept and understand a situation before we can seek to change it. While we are blinded, however, we will remain blinded and continue to manifest the same outcomes. But, once we can see a situation for what it is, we can change our own behavior and, thus, forever change its outcome.

As a means for soul growth, Life has a way of presenting us with opportunities to learn lessons. These lessons will repeat until we change our response to these lessons. But first, amidst the lesson, it is helpful to realize and be grateful for the lesson itself. Once we do, it becomes easy to change our usual responses. Some call it growth...others refer to it as a lesson learned.

The Law of Patience & Reward

Goodness returns to those who put out good. The Great Law tells us that. But, we must do so with patience and a humble heart. God instructs us to live our purpose in love and faithfulness. So, toil on. Focus steadfast on your goal. The reward will come. It is Law.

The Law of Significance & Inspiration

The amount of intent and energy one puts into an action directly correlates to the amount and strength of energy received from it. That for which we give the highest loving energy will produce the greatest returns. Simply speaking, we get out of Life that which we put into it. This is part of the reason why it's so important that we find our God-given passion. Through our passions, we are naturally inspired so, working on them isn't considered "working" at all. Yet, we will still reap the highest rewards due to the amount of genuinely loving energy used to achieve them.

CHAPTER 8

A BEAUTEOUS LIFE

If there is one guiding idea that should be taken from this book, that idea is LOVE. Love everyone and everything. Every life is precious and must be valued and appreciated. So, it is imperative that we respond with the most loving response to all situations. For, Love is who we are…we need only to remember and exhibit it.

Right now, I am at a phenomenal point in my life. I am magnificently blessed to have an astounding Love…the love from my wife and family. Every day I awaken with such joy in my heart for them. I appreciate each one of them for the fantastically silly, smart, courageous, talented, strong, and beautiful people they each are. They are my world and I thank God every day for answering my deepest silent prayer…to have a family of my own. Having been raised by older parents plus my grandmother, all three of my parental figures had passed by the time I was in my mid-thirties. So, I felt alone in this world for many years. To finally have a family that loves me is priceless. And, my heart is warmer than it has ever been.

I am excited about the future and believe that only good things are coming my way because God has cleared the way. And, for this, I am most grateful. I live a beautiful life because I see beauty in all things. It is my hope that every life on this planet sees beauty in every instance and reveres in awe at the magnificence of God.

I thank every reader for sharing in my experience and hope that the Divinings shared throughout this book can resonate within each of your hearts. We are amidst of a cosmic elevation of consciousness, Friends. And, many right now are evolving into enlightened beings. To those, I say have patience with yourselves during this process and stay forever grateful and humble. This journey is often arduous. But, by remembering to consciously view each situation from a higher view, we will understand our behavior and grow. And, all growth, no matter how small the step forward may seem, is actually a grand leap in consciousness. Embrace any forward motion. I genuinely love all of you and soulfully send the world outspreading and outpouring energetic Light during every interaction. Again, I thank you and humbly bow to the inner you that resides in each of us. Be well, Friends.

Through God's Infinite Light and Wisdom,
I will do my part to raise the collective awareness of all humanity.

www.ingramcontent.com/pod-product-compliance
Lightning Source LLC
Chambersburg PA
CBHW051736040426
42447CB00008B/1164